Home is further away

比闪电还远的是故乡

than the lightning

Home is further away
比闪电还远的是故乡
than the lightning

Zhang Chunhua

translated by
Ouyang Yu

PUNCHER & WATTMANN

© Zhang Chunhua 2022
Translation © Ouyang Yu 2022

This book is copyright. Apart from any fair dealing for the purposes of study and research, criticism, review or as otherwise permitted under the Copyright Act, no part may be reproduced by any process without written permission. Inquiries should be made to the publisher.

First published in 2022
Published by Puncher and Wattmann
PO Box 279
Waratah NSW 2298

http://www.puncherandwattmann.com
puncherandwattmann@bigpond.com

ISBN   9781922571175

Cover design by Morgan Arnett
Printed by Lightning Source International

 A catalogue record for this book is available from the National Library of Australia

Contents

宇宙墙	11	The Wall of the Universe
橙汁加冰	13	Orange Juice with Ice
生物钟	15	Biological Clock
K次元的骰子	17	Dice for Dimension K
锁孔背后	19	Behind the Keyhole
有一些词才刚刚诞生	21	Words, Just Born
黑色素	23	The Black Pigment
选择失忆	25	Selective Amnesia
春天的花园	27	The Garden in Spring
比闪电还远的是故乡	29	Home Is Further Away than the Lightning
坐标系	31	A Coordinate System
假如月亮转过身来	33	If the Moon Turned Around
吸盘	35	The Sucker
末日展	37	An Exhibition of the End of the Day
思想的花园	39	A Garden of Thoughts
意识对物质的变奏（组诗）	41	Variation of Consciousness on Matter (A Sequence)
绿棉袄	55	The Green Cotton Jacket
温室效应	57	Greenhouse Effect
漂流瓶	59	The Drifting Bottle
撕裂	61	Tearing
燃烧	63	Burning
弯曲的不仅仅是地上的河流	65	It's Not Only the Rivers That Are Bent
着陆器	67	The Landing Vehicle
我无法拒绝你的到来	69	I Can't Refuse Your Coming
虫子的哲学	71	The Philosophy of an Insect
中文房间	73	A Room of Chinese Language
行走在黑暗里的钟	75	The Clock Walking in the Darkness
无法阻挡	77	Impossible to Stop
渐行渐远	79	Getting Further Away

链接 还在继续	81	The Link, Still Continuing
玩具屋	83	The Dollhouse
猫的脚步比时间的钟摆还轻	85	The Cat's Steps Always Lighter than the Pendulum
总想 爱这个世界多一点	87	Always Wanting to Love This World a Bit More
伸出你的手	89	Hold Out Your Hands
光年系列·圣杯	91	Holy Grail • the Light Year Series
光年系列·起始	93	The Beginnings • the Light Year Series
开始融化	95	Beginning to Melt
有一双眼睛停在我的左脸	97	There Was a Pair of Eyes Stopped on My Face
你一直在哪里	99	Where Have You Been?
物质的边沿	101	At the Edge of the Matter
剥开一枚果壳	103	Opening the Shell of a Fruit
我弯曲地寄生在你肉体的深处	105	I, Bent, Lived in the Depths of Your Body, Like a Parasite
梦山	107	The Dream Mountain
远方走来一位失明的歌者	109	A Blind Singer Came from Afar
她的盛装还是那样艳丽	111	Her Finery Was Still So Gorgeous
核	113	Nuclear

About the Author

Zhang Chunhua, also known by his penname Youfu Shidai (Age of UFO), was born in 1963 in Nanchang, Jiangxi. Now living in Shanghai, he has had his work published in such anthologies as *Excellent Poems in the China Internet Poetry Front for Comments and Appreciation*, *A Selection of Poetry in Grain Rain: Thirty Years of Poetry in Jiangxi*, *Best-selling Chinese Poetry in 2012*, *Best Poems of Jiangxi in the 21st Century*, *A File of New Chinese Poetry*, *Selected Poetry Monthly*, *Shanghai Poets*, *Best-selling Chinese Poems in 2018*, *An Annual Collection of Chinese Poetry in 2017*, *The 2019 New Chinese Poetry Calendar*, *International Chinese-language Poetry*, *The West*, and *Prism 2018: An International Collection of Poetry in Multiple Languages* (in India). He has published one book of poetry, *Temperature*, and was invited to The Seventh International Poetry Festival in Malaysia in 2016.

张春华，（笔名：幽浮时代），1963年生，江西南昌人，现居上海，部分作品入选《中国网络诗歌前沿佳作评赏》、《谷雨诗选：江西诗歌三十年》、《2012年中国诗歌排行榜》、《21世纪江西诗歌精选》、《中华新诗档案》，以及《诗选刊》、《上海诗人》、《2018年中国新诗排行榜》、《2017中国诗歌年选》、《2019年中国新诗日历》、《国际汉语诗歌》、《西部》《棱镜2018-国际多语种诗歌选集》（印度）等境内、外报刊、网刊、杂志，出版个人诗集《体温》，应邀参加2016年马来西亚第七届国际诗歌节。

宇宙墙

天使的翅膀变得沉重起来
密集的陨石的雨点 缓慢坠落
我在一颗遥远的蓝色之星
感知到又一个旧纪元的崩溃

我的呼吸与银河的星系同步
我和微尘一道附在泥土的肌肤上
我的脉搏仅保留时间的痕迹
我光年的穹顶 是我象限的归宿

黑暗与光的搏杀仍在继续
重生的气泡在宇宙的体内漫延
恒星的斑点扩展至我苍白的脸庞
血液与滚石同命运相互交织

万物的触角停滞在引力边沿
一块苍穹是鸟儿无法逾越的高远
一片海洋 是鱼无穷的湛蓝
一段流火 是星辰疼痛的一瞬

(2019.2.16)

The Wall of the Universe

The wings of the angels have become heavy
As the raindrops of dense meteorites   slowly fall
In a far, blue star, I feel
The collapse of another old era

My breathings synchronized with the galaxy
Fine dust and I, we stick to the skin of the mud
My pulse keeps tracks only of time's traces
While the dome of my light years   is the quadrant of my destination

The fight between darkness and light is continuing
Bubbles of rebirth are permeating in the body of the universe
Spots of the planet are expanding to my pale face
While blood and rolling stones are interwoven with the fate

Tentacles of things have stopped at the edge of gravitation
A block of sky is the high-far that birds can't go beyond
A spread of the ocean   is the boundless blue for the fish
A section of the flowing fire   an instant of the stars' pain

橙汁加冰

单纯的物质魅力
是来自于默然的偶合与遭遇
直至摄魂的幻化成另一个
迷一样的自我
无法逃脱的
是摆在面前捕获你影子的镜面
连穿透一阵劲风的光线
也要接受折煞 或重叠的事实

当然世界的相加会继续 包括
仇恨与苦难的相加
爱与背叛的相加
思念与回不去的故土的相加
莫名的是一种柔性的相加
深入到另一种硬质的相加的内部
脱变出疯长的锯齿物
其中橙色的甜蜜 已支离破碎

(2018.7.18)

Orange Juice with Ice

The glamour of matter, pure and simple
Comes from the coupling and encounter of silence
Till, spellbound, it turns into another
Self, like a mystery
What is inescapable
Is the mirror, in front of you, that captures your shadow
Even the light that penetrates a strong wind
Will have to accept facts   that are unbearable or overlapped

Of course, the additions of the world will continue   including
Those of hatred and suffering
Those of love and betrayal
Those of longing and the native land one can't return to
What can't be named is the addition of a softness
That goes deep into the inside of an addition of another hardness
And turns into a madly growing saw-toothed matter
Its orange-coloured sweetness   having fragmented

生物钟

神的手　无法触摸到
它柔软的指针　它是宇宙脉搏的一部分
是这颗星球黑暗里的心跳

浩瀚之海　凶险的
波涛下　有均匀而美妙的读秒声
奏响这深蓝的时光曲

它在星光之前
与晨露的起落同步　它一路紧随
雪山飞狐　草原之鹰

它走过青铜时代
冲破铁器与白银时代的绞杀　它精确的
计算着你死的过去　生的未来

(2018.6.4)

Biological Clock

The deity's hands   can't reach
Its soft pointers   part of the universe's pulse
The leaping of a heart inside the darkness of this planet

Under the dangerous   vastness
Of the ocean   there is the reading of seconds, even and beautiful
That plays the time's melody in the deep blue

Prior to the starlight, it
Synchronizes with the rise and fall of the morning dew   all the way following
The flying fox on the snowy mountain   and the eagle over the grassland

It crosses the Age of Bronze
Breaking through the strangulation of iron with white silver   it accurately
Calculating the past of your death   the future of your life

K 次元的骰子

死亡 是一连串数字
和符号的熄灭 是闪烁和跳动恢复平静
掌握与嵌入密钥的手
在抚慰创伤时
也在激活更凶狠的连接

你无法寻找黑暗前的影子
每一次来 都是一场重新的编排
每一次的回忆 都是再现上一回的绝决
撕扯完冷却的肉身
你会一路伴随闪灵 逃离天域之城的边沿

除了光的锁链 还有星辰的起落
谁来选定魔方翻转的次数
在有机的妩媚和无机的刚毅之间
带水晶皇冠的胜利者
将重置 另一个 K 次元的骰子

(2018.5.23)

Dice for Dimension K

Death   is a series of numbers
And extinguished signs   is flickerings and jumpings recovering peace
The hands that master the secret keys, embedded in them
Fondle the wounds
As they activate even more ferocious connections

You can't search for the shadows prior to darkness
Every come   is a re-arrangement
Every memory   is a re-presentation of the finality last time
After tearing off the cooled body
You'll run away from the edges of the sky-edge city   with the flashing spirit
                                                                           in company all the way

Apart from the chains of light   there is also the rise and fall of the stars
Who will decide on the number of turns Rubik's Cube is subject to?
Between the organic charming and the inorganic hardihood
The victor with a crystal crown
Will re-set   a dice for another Dimension K

锁孔背后

是一个微缩的空间
是隔阂之后 怯懦的存在

从这个孔 向外窥探
除了淋漓的风雨 还有一束
射向背后凶冷的光

在历史有篱笆的年代
纸张上的故事 变得扑朔迷离
悬念反转 没有预设时间表

暗物质 继续纠缠白天和黑夜
也纠缠游走的魂魄
死寂过后 锁孔会沉重的关闭

(2017.12.3)

Behind the Keyhole

Is a micro space
a timid existence　　after the estrangement

looking outside　　through this hole
apart from the dripping wind and rain　　there is also a bunch
of cold and hard lights that are shot at the back

in history, in the years with the fences
stories on paper　　become blurry
suspensions reversed　　no pre-set timetables

dark matter　　continuing to beset the days and nights
and to entangle the ghosts drifting away
after the dead silence　　the keyhole will close heavily

有一些词才刚刚诞生

老的词
与老的协约 老的城邦一起
早已死在 老的字典或老的古籍里

新的世界
混杂在不同肤色和喉咙的喊杀声中
字母与笔画相互搏击

有一些词才刚刚诞生
根本来不及呐喊和穿戴整齐
便倒在失守的边界

逃亡的思绪
一路奔腾 越过海洋 陆地 星空
我成为流放的单词

(2017.3.15)

Words, Just Born

Old words
are together with old agreements   old cities
long dead   in old dictionaries or old classics

a new world
mixed with the battle-cry of different skin colours and throats
letters and radicals fighting with each other

words, just born
with no time to shout and get dressed
before they fall on the border that has lost its guards

the escaping thoughts
are rushing all the way   across the ocean   the land   the starry sky
and I have become a word in exile

黑色素

我击败调色盘里的三原色
向唇与乳的边沿扩散
释放出成熟的吞噬世界的魔力

透过皮肤和毛孔
我想告诉　　稚嫩的红
和单纯的即将死去的蓝

我是太阳之子
在千万次的裂变中感知光和热
让细胞和血起舞　　涌动

我是精灵　　从撒哈拉到科罗拉多
我的每一寸肌肤上
都能找到大地与阳光的影子

(2013.5.18)

The Black Pigment

I defeated the three primary colours on the palette
as I dispersed from the edge of the lips and nipples
giving forth a mature magic power in swallowing up the world

through the skin and the pores
I'd like to tell   of the tender red
and the dying blue that was pure

I, son of the sun
have felt the light and heat in the disintegrations of millions of times
letting the cells and blood dance   and surge

I am a spirit   from the Sahara to Colorado
every inch of my skin
capable of finding the shadow of the land and the sun

选择失忆

当苦痛与罪恶于白天降临时
我会在寂静的夜 选择失忆

除了部分没有玷污的爱恋
还有马尔克斯 有关行刑队的消息

我知道这世界 耗费了100年
来校对各种兵器的精度与强度

冷血的生命在残喘 并潜在海底或地下
热血的勇士以主义或国家的名誉射杀

我的北方 一道陨石
划破摩尔曼斯克的夜空

其实 愤怒的天神已经昏睡
拾荒者的眼与猫眼相视 闪出白光

我的脑海里 清晰的画面在消逝
连同一丝温暖也变得模糊起来

(2014.4.20)

Selective Amnesia

When pain and sin fall on the day
I shall select amnesia   in the stillness of a night

Except for love that is partially not polluted
And Marquez's news   about the death squad

I know that this world   has squandered 100 years
In calibrating the accuracy and strength of all sorts of weaponry

Cold-blood lives are lingering on feebly   hidden underground or at the
                                                                               bottom of the sea
While hot-blood warriors are killing in the name of isms or nations

My north   a meteorite
That crosses the night sky over Murmansk

Whereas in fact   the angry God has gone asleep
The scavenger is eying the eyes of a cat   flashing white

In my brain   the clear picture is disappearing
Becoming obscure, along with a thread of warmth

春天的花园

在一个垃圾堆满春天的花园里
充足的肥料和富氧的空气
催生出一朵朵极艳的花
鬼魅而潮湿的南风
喜欢在这个园子的中央徘徊
并逗夜色脱光超大的黑幕的裤子时
强奸其中最高挑的一朵
在获得一阵摇摆的快感后迅速逃离现场
留下满地残败的落红　　可这
仅是春天的第一个晚上发生的事情

(2014.4.30)

The Garden in Spring

In a garden in which rubbish fills the spring
Sufficient manure and the air, rich in oxygen
Bring forth ravishing flowers
The ghostly and wet southern wind
Likes to pace, to and fro, in the middle of this garden
And rape the tallest flower
When the night takes off the pants of the extra-large black screen
Running away from the scene after gaining a swaying pleasure
With the ground covered in fallen red   but this
Is only what happened on the first night of the spring

比闪电还远的是故乡

光与影 轮番消磨我的肉身
属于我的灵魂
开始 寻找另一条通道或出口

银河的边沿
有一颗停泊的母星 等待我的归期
连接是一束简短的密语

已经过滤的罪恶
和彻底放下的苦难
恢宏的庙宇 十字的塔顶可以证明

始终缠绕在一起的是兄弟 姐妹
拥挤的世界有过风 有过雨 有过思恋
比闪电还远的是故乡

(2016.7.17)

Home Is Further Away than the Lightning

Light and shadow   wears down my body, by turns
the soul that belongs to me
began   looking for another access or exit

the edge of the galaxy
has a mother star moored   waiting for my return
the connection being a bunch of secret codes

the sin, already filtered
and the misery, thoroughly put down
can be proven by the cross on the top of the tower   and the magnificent temple

those who remain entangled with each other   are siblings
the crowded world had wind   rain   longings
home is further away than the lightning

坐标系

起初 我在这个空间
属于没有重量的影子
当我还处在零的时候
纯净和空蒙
只知道用幻觉去猜测星光

我拥有的世界
既不是存在 也不是虚无
总之前方有路 路无限
面对永恒的时光
苦难无边 幸福也无边
一旦我的呼吸弥漫开来
不知是轻 还是重
只感到属于我的生命开始舞蹈

事物开始无情地按单位记数
有时克 有时秒
天空在旋转 我却静止
或曲线 或直线   或汪洋一片
尽管我单薄的足印浪迹天涯
总有知己和我一一对应
不是在水一方 就是在路之遥

即使我累了   悄然离去
所有的象限不再有我的轨迹
也不会黯然伤神   我从零而来
注定要回到零哪儿去
找回我的纯净 我的空蒙

(2008.4.20)

A Coordinate System

In the beginning   I, in this space
was a mere weightless shadow
when I was at zero
pure and empty
I only knew to guess about the starlight with my illusions

the world I owned
was no existence   nor was it vacuity
all in all, there was a road   a limitless road
in front of eternity
misery was boundless   happiness was also boundless
once my breathing permeated
I knew not whether it was light   or heavy
I only knew that life that belonged to me began dancing

things began ruthlessly recording the unit-based numbers
grams sometimes   seconds at other times
the sky was gyrating   but I kept still
lines, curved or straight   or the vastness of an ocean
although my thin footprints reached the end of the earth
there was always someone who knew me to respond to me
in the far road   if not on the other side of the river

if I was tired   and left quietly
none of the quadrants would bear my traces
nor would they feel sad   as I've come from zero
and am bound to return there
to find back my purity   and my emptiness

假如月亮转过身来

每年中秋　皓月当空时　我在想
月亮会不会转过身来
当然这是一个永远不可能发生的事情

某一年真的发生　广寒宫的嫦娥仙子
和桂花树　转到了月亮背面
从未露出尊容的另一面便显现出来

这个至今　依然漆黑的迷
连唐时的李白　宋时的东坡
也不敢想象　映入眼帘的是丑还是美

或许杀出一支舰队来　摆脱束缚
直奔地球　为表示友好
我在阳台贡上月饼　待天兵天将降临

(2015.9.27)

If the Moon Turned Around

Every mid-autumn night   when the bright moon hangs in the sky   I wonder
If the moon will not turn around
But, of course, that is not something that will happen

Once, though   this did happen when Chang'e the Fairy
And the laurel tree   turned to the other side of the moon
Its other side, never shown before, now revealed

This mystery   that remains dark to this day
Is something neither Li Bai in the Tang dynasty   nor Su Shi in the Song
Dared imagine   as ugly or beautiful

Perhaps a fleet of frigates might rush out   of its bondage
Towards Earth   and to express my friendship
I present moon cakes in my balcony   to await the descendance of the sky soldiers

吸盘

有吸盘的肢体　其实
是一段没有思想与痛楚的生命
只为牢牢地守护　　　而活着

无论是尖锐的　或是有毒的深渊
都要面对　　　并靠得更近
甚至让视线里的空气凝固成锁

当然心会停止跳动　　色彩也会
躲进黑暗里　　　　　不过
你灵魂的吸附将枯萎成一朵海石花

(2013.9.6)

The Sucker

Limbs with suckers   in fact
Are sections of a life without thought and pain
Alive   for the purpose of holding onto something fast

The abyss, sharp   or poisonous
Has to face   and get close
To even allow the air in the line of sight to congeal

But the heart will surely stop beating   and the colours will also
Hide themselves in the darkness   although
The sucking of your soul will wither into a coral flower

末日展

庞贝的最后一天
太阳　在正午1点钟的时候开始陨落

所有的神　面对维苏威的火焰
均沉默不语

连通向天堂的门　也重重关闭了
腾起的松树状的云朵　成为此时此刻的主宰

当然　后面是来不及分享的今日的晚宴
和无法抵达的情人的幽会

财富和荣耀　贫穷和坠落
凝固在这一堆厚厚的死灰中　竟二千年没变

我的无语与沉默告诉我
地动山摇的事实　始终藏匿在这颗星球的内心深处

(2016.10.7)

An Exhibition of the End of the Day

Last day in Pompeii
The sun   began setting at 1 p.m.

All the deities   in front of the fire of Vesuvius
Kept silent

Even the gate to heaven   had heavily closed
The cloud, surging in the shape of a pine   was now dominating the moment

Of course   what followed was dinner tonight one had no time to share
And the meeting with lovers one could hardly reach

Fortune and glory   poverty and fall
All frozen in the heap of thick dead ashes   unchanged in the last two
                                                              thousand years

My wordlessness and my silence told me
An earth-moving fact   eternally hidden in the depths of this planet's heart

思想的花园

01

在思想的花园
经常有人悬梁自尽
他们是　斗士　求索者　勇士　诗人　优秀青年

02

我从来没有数过
这座城里到底有多少个拐角
和多少堵墙　只知道地下的管子比肠子还长
从马路的这头
通向马路的哪头　无穷无尽

03

一群蚂蚁　迎着落日排队回家
经过大理石窗台　发现提前回家的同伴尸横遍野
一瓶高大的枪手牌气雾剂　摆在
离洞穴二米的地方

04

我能感到偷窥者的心跳
和一双带刺的眼睛
紧贴后背　镶嵌在空气里
在人民广场转了一圈　也没摆脱掉

(2018.8.22)

A Garden of Thoughts

01

In the garden of thoughts
people frequently hang themselves
they are fighters   seekers   warriors   poets   fine youths

02

I have never counted
how many corners there are in this city
and how many walls   all I know is that the pipelines underground are
                                            longer than the intestines
from this end of the road
to that end   it's endless

03

A team of ants   going home in the face of the setting sun
past the granite windowsill   when they find it strewn with their companions'
                                                                      corpses
an aerosol, Gunman, big and tall   is placed
two metres away from the cave

04

I can feel the heart beatings of a voyeur
and a pair of piercing eyes
sticking onto my back   embedded in the air
I didn't manage to get rid of it   even though I covered People's Square in
                                                                one circle

意识对物质的变奏（组诗）

沙子 是死了的泥土

山鸡在嘲笑鸡的时候
总是把自己看成 鹰

眼睛看到的真理 往往
被大脑 贱卖给了嘴

茶沏的过程 是
叶的僵尸复活的过程

鱼在水里看到的星星 是
天空睾丸中的几粒 鱼籽

风 走过河塘 再走过每一扇窗
但它从不告诉你 野鸭
当着荷花的面 偷欢的故事

马有一天尿急 发明了马桶
奇怪 马自己从来就没用过

思想家在形成思想之前 有如
花生仁 在花生之前那样简单

小河知道自己永远见不到海 但
愿意千万次的 死在去海的路上

镜片先于眼睛看到真相 却
受到尘埃　　一次又一次干扰

Variation of Consciousness on Matter (A Sequence)

Sands   dead mud

When a mountain chicken laughs at a chicken
It always regards itself as   an eagle

The truth the eyes see   often
Is sold cheap by the brain   to the mouth

The making of tea   is
A process in which a corpse comes alive

The stars the fish see in the water   are
A few fish eggs   in the testicles of the sky

The wind   walks across the river pond   past all the windows
But it never tells you   of how the wild ducks
Seek pleasure in front of the lotus flowers

The horse got urgent wanting to piss one day   so the horse barrel was invented
Strange it is   that the horses never use them

Before a thinker formed his thought   it was
As simple as the kernel   inside the peanut

The small river knows that it won't see the ocean   but
It is willing to die   on its way there, for thousands of times

The glasses see the truth before the eye   but
Get interference   again and again from the dust

宠物 是绝育后的野兽

一支人马屠杀另一支人马
一群蚂蚁咬死另一群蚂蚁
前者为国王 后者为蚁王

钻石做梦都没想到 死了一万年 还能
同天下 所有最富最美的新娘同眠共枕

太空宣判 行走的死亡
为无牵无挂的永恒开路

秋天是夏天的结果
也是 冬天的乳娘

狼 最后一次嚎叫
才是 鬼哭的声音

警察腰间的警棍　在站街女
眼里　不如她的舌尖有力

用领子的颜色区别口袋里的钞票
好比用垃圾的分类区别垃圾

轻轻波涛 在海风的劝说下
走向岸 没想到被岩石撕得粉碎

故乡 是大多数灵魂的产地

贫穷的种子　在花天酒地中
萌生的芽最毒

A pet   is a sterilized animal

A team of people butchers another team
A team of ants eat another team
The first becomes the king   the second: the Ant King

Diamond has never dreamt that   in ten thousand years it can
Sleep with the richest and the most beautiful brides in the world

Space has announced that   the walking death
Must make a pathway for the constraint-less eternity

Autumn, fruit of the summer
Is also   the nanny of the winter

When the wolf   howls for a last time
It sounds   like a devil

The baton in the belt of a policeman   in the eyes of
A streetwalker   is not as powerful as the tip of her tongue

When you tell the banknotes in your pocket from the colour of your collar
It's like telling the rubbish from the categories of rubbish

Light waves   persuaded by the sea wind
Walk towards the bank   but are torn into pieces by the rocks

Home   source of most souls

Seeds of poverty   in liquor land
Sprout the most poisonous buds

帆　一边与船厮守
一边与风　谈婚论嫁

纪念的日子活着是因为在心里
纪念的日子死了是因为在墙上

用眼泪杀人的不一定是　鳄鱼
用嘴招来灾祸的不一定是乌鸦

一个普通木箱　摆在庙里叫
功德箱　摆在街上叫垃圾箱

玫瑰　伤人之前迷人
罂粟迷人之后　伤人

弓出卖箭时　弦是帮凶

痛苦是灵魂走得太快　身体走得太慢
快乐　是身体一边工作灵魂一边安息

因极端　一次又一次爱上主义
仇恨　便一次又一次猎杀人性

水被水管肢解　分尸后
其最大的死亡是　不死

长大的　是快乐或痛苦
长不大的是摇篮及乳臭

鸟儿回来了　还有歌声
先在心里　然后在树上

Sails   cling to the boat
While discussing the possibility of marriage   with the wind

Memorial days are kept alive only in the heart
And they are dead because they are on the wall

Those who kill with tears are not necessarily   crocodiles
And those who court disasters with their mouths are not necessarily   crows

An ordinary wooden box   is called Virtue Box
When placed in a temple   but it is called Rubbish Box, placed on a street

Roses   attractive before they hurt
Poppies   hurt after they attract people

When the bow sells the arrow   the string is an accomplice

Painful because the soul walks too fast   and the body, too slow
Happiness   body working as soul takes a rest

Because of extremes   one falls in love with ism again and again
And because of hatred   one repetitively kills

Water, when dismembered and split up by the waterpipes
Its maximum death is   non-death

What grows up   is happiness or pain
What can't grow up is the cradle and the smell of the baby

Birds come back   with the song
First in the heart   then in the trees

门嘲笑锁 是贼的计谋

蚂蚁请小姐按摩 最大的错误
是选择了指压 没有选择脚踩

懒散的阳光 躺在
现实的长椅上 照样会枯死

神父在咽气的前一分钟 才
发现 上帝从来没讲过真话

印第安人的祖国埋在神庙下
毛利人的祖国被彻底 偷走
扔石头的兄弟 你的祖国呢？

人们只在失去果实时 才想起种子

在秘密的花园里 唯有蛇
可以享受 毒蘑菇的鲜美

人 从虎的眼睛里看到残存的威严
虎从人的眼睛中看到 绝对的贪婪

最傻的蚊子 也不会在厚厚的冬天复活
最蠢的苍蝇都知道在厕所与餐厅的距离

魔鬼在成为魔鬼之前也善良过 如
垃圾在成为垃圾之前也高贵过一样

当爱说服了性时
情不一定属于你的生活

The door laughs at the lock   for being the stratagem of a thief

When an ant asks a working girl for massage   the worst mistake it makes
Is it's chosen the finger pressure   not the foot tread

The lazy sunlight   lying
On the bench of reality   will be withered to death as usual

It's not till one minute before the priest breathes his last   that he
Finds out that   God has never told the truth

The motherland of the Indians is buried below a sacred temple
And that of the Maoris, thoroughly   stolen
What about yours   stone-throwers, my brothers?

It's not till people have lost their fruit   that they begin remembering the seeds

In a secret garden   only the snake
Can enjoy   the freshness of the poisonous mushrooms

People can see   the majesty remaining in the eyes of a tiger
But the tiger can only see   the absolute greed in the eyes of a man

Even the most stupid mosquitoes   wont' come alive in the thick winter
And even the most stupid flies know the distance between a toilet and a dining room

The devil was good before it became the devil   the same way
Rubbish was noble before it turned into rubbish

When love convinces sex
Feelings do not necessarily belong to your life

粪球 在屎克郎的眼里不是粪球
自然在自然的法则面前才是珍爱

饱餐过后的幽灵 每次在马路上溜达
最怕撞上 三天没有进过食的流浪狗

一口枯井完全能够证明 已经
失去的比现在获得的 还珍贵

蝶 在蛹的时候没想到过飞翔
生命的起步 从希望开始成长

我的血脉的源头 在我的祖国
我为之交出我的全部是应该的

梦的故事感人 且惊怵而甜美
不过是灵魂的一场虚无的彩排

珠峰 你可以不断征服我绝对的高度
但征服不了 日益膨胀的欲望的高度

雷电谈不上是宇宙之剑发出的光芒 因
孕育雷电的云 不过是星河中的一缕纱

蚊子听吸血鬼授课
从不打瞌睡

一种思想总是在反对
另一种思想时才光芒四射

癞蛤蟆想 走夜路不一定
碰到鬼 也许能碰到天使

Balls of shit   remain balls of shit in the eyes of a beetle
But nature is loved only in front of natural law

Every time the ghost, well fed   strolls on the street
It is most afraid of   bumping into a stray dog that has not eaten anything for 3 days

A dry well can fully testify   that it has
Lost much more treasure than it   has now gained

The butterfly   does not think of flying when it's in the chrysalis
The same way life starts   by growing with hope

The source of my blood   is in my motherland
So I ought to give it all I have

The story of the dream is moving   amazingly sweet
But it's just a dress rehearsal of the soul

The Everest   you can keep conquering my absolute height
But you can't overcome   the height of my daily swelling desire

You can't describe lightning as the light of the sword in the universe   because
The clouds breeding it   are a thread of gauze in the river of stars

Mosquitoes, when attending the class, run by the blood-sucking devil
Never fall asleep

Only when one thought is opposed to another
That the other thought shines with brilliance

The toad is thinking   if I walk the road by night
I might run into an angel   instead of a devil

天宇只所以茫茫　是无穷的思想
被困在有限的长度里　不能自拔

可卡因嘲笑鸦片老了　K粉开始登场
梦幻般地摇着青春的头

河的确是在鱼被杀的前一天死的　卵石
在造物主面前　讲述一起谋杀案的经过

长大了才知道不是亲娘的奶水比乳娘
的少　是乳娘的心胸比亲娘的心胸纯厚

发明旗帜的人或许是位舞者　是为
实现飘扬　并迎着风向前的感觉

胡须摆脱不了被刮的命运　是
因为　他离主人说谎的嘴太近

异性拥有的是暗香之后的灿烂
同性欣赏的是烈艳过后的孤独

医生的谎言　往往会比
真理的谎言更具说服力

农夫和渔夫进城务工最大的收获
不是金钱　是金钱背后的出卖或被出卖

当　英雄的血流干的时候
英雄的故事才刚刚　开始

蚂蚁过马路时从不走斑马的线
金鱼游了一生还是死在玻璃里

The universe is vast   because the boundless thoughts
Are stuck in the limited length   unable to pull themselves out

Cocaine laughs at the opium for being old   when Ketamine steps onto the stage
Dreamily shaking its youthful head

The river did die one day before the fish were killed   when the pebbles
Recounted how   the murder took place

It's only when one grows up that one knows one's blood mother's milk
Is less than the nanny's   but that the nanny's bosoms are broader

The inventor of a flag may be a dancer   for the purpose
Of making it flutter   and experiencing the forwardness of it in the wind

Moustache can't escape the fate of being shaved   because
It is too close   to the mouth of the liar

What one of the opposite sex owns is the brilliance after the hidden fragrance
Whereas the same sex enjoys the solitude after cruising

A doctor's lies   are often more
Persuasive than the lies of a truth

The most gain a peasant and a fisherman make in the city
Is not money   but betrayal behind the money or being betrayed

When   the blood of a hero dries up
That's when his story has just   begun

When the ants cross a street, they never take the zebra crossing
And when the golden fish swims for a whole life, it still dies inside the glass bowl

灰尘与吸尘器的斗争从未停止过
只是每一次都是以彻底的失败而告终

冷兵器与热兵器交手 前者
闪光的锋利 挡不住后者无影的穿透

刽子手下地狱后
做的第一件事是隐姓埋名

一只候鸟站在空难的现场发呆
是禽流感？还是偷猎？

倒下 这个词在树的字典里没有
在人的字典可以找到

鱼在想 你们的男女之欢和我们
的鱼水之欢 根本就不是一回事

(2009.6.6 – 2015.10.1)

The fight between dust and a vacuum cleaner never stops
Except that it ends always in being thoroughly defeated

When cold weapons and hot weapons come to blows   the shiny sharpness
Of the former   can't stop the shadowless penetration of the latter

After the executioner goes to hell
The first thing he does is to be anonymous

A bird of passage stands in the site of an air crash, stupefied
Is that the bird flu? Or poaching?

To fall   this expression is not findable in a dictionary of trees
It is, in a dictionary of people

The fish are thinking   the pleasure between you men and women
Are totally different   from the pleasure between us water and fish

绿棉袄

这是 一位祖母
为自己亲手准备的庄重的仪式的一部分
紧接着是准备黑裤子
和一双薄的不能行走的蓝底小缎鞋

窗外雨露的水形 始终
保持晶莹的周而复始的秩序
时光偷偷潜伏在祖母斑驳的发际 一串
陌生的耳语 来自星光的指引

奇丽的颜色
会融入夜晚的天空之城
且覆盖掉曾行走过的苍白的小径 何时
乡村和原野变得模糊起来

眼睛可触摸的事物
在广柔的暗物质的疆域里
会尽情彩排着最后那一段美丽的姿势
此刻 祖母的身影便在其中

(2019.7.14)

The Green Cotton Jacket

This is   part of a solemn ritual a grandmother
has prepared for herself with her own hands
closely followed by her preparation for a pair of black trousers
and a small pair of blue-soled satin shoes, so thin one can't walk in them

the watery shape of rain dew outside the window   constantly
keeps its repeated crystalline order
while time, by stealth, hides at Grandma's mottled hairline   a string
of strange whispers   come from the guidance of the starlight

colours, singularly beautiful
may merge into the city of the sky at night
and cover up the pale path, walked on once, from when
the village and the plain have become obscured?

things that can be touched by the eye
in the region of vastly soft dark matter
will do their best to rehearse the last beautiful posture
and, right now, Grandma's figure is in it

温室效应

  地球不属于我
  而我属于地球

   - 印第安酋长

你的油轮继续通过连接两个大洋的海峡
你岸上的巨炮继续紧盯深蓝水面
你粉色的沙暴 继续席卷着整个阿拉伯海
你极地的冰熊继续漂在浮冰上

你湿地的呕吐 继续沾满亚马逊的阔叶
你电锯的痉挛继续成为一阵粗壮的枝干的反抗
你街区的黑色灵车继续阻塞在三层立交
你流火的唾液继续漫过笨重而肥厚的肩胛

你继续在露天操场用强日光直接刺杀掉性别
你继续在玻璃中繁衍 寄生出优雅而舒适的胚胎
你继续等待的蜂与花的种子 崩溃在巢穴里
你继续回望的白垩纪最后一夜 死星划过天空

(2019.6.24)

Greenhouse Effect

The Earth does not belong to me
But I belong to it

— An American-Indian Chief

Your oil tanker keeps passing through the channel connecting the two oceans
Your huge cannons keep staring over the deep-blue water surfaces
Your pink storm   keeps engulfing the Arabian Sea
And your polar bears keep floating on the broken ices

The vomiting of your wetland   keeps staining the broad leaves of Amazon
The convulsions of your electric saw keep becoming the rebellion of thick boughs
The black hearse of your block keeps blocking at the three-tier exchange
The spit of your flowing fire keeps flowing over the stupid and fat shoulder-blades

You keep directly killing gender with strong sunlight in the playground
You keep breeding in the glass   parasitizing elegant and comfortable embryos
The seeds of bees and flowers you keep awaiting   have collapsed in the cave
And on the last night of the Cretaceous Period you keep looking back to   a dead
                                                                star crossing the sky

漂流瓶

1886 你把它投进海里

写上一句纯净的话语和遥远的问候
你的孤独和你的大陆
便有一种寄托 你
刚好 停在马车和木帆船时代

自东日本海出发
沿太平洋暖流至美国西海岸
再到曝晒的布里斯班
长条的塑料的岛屿 正在
集结 向南擦过
那个一百年前投下的漂流瓶

此刻 从宋卡府传来
一头鲸鱼吞食 80 个塑料袋 死在
安达曼海域的消息

(2019.6.15)

The Drifting Bottle

In 1886   you chucked it into the sea
with a pure word   and greetings from a faraway place
your loneliness and your continent
then had a resting place   you
happened to be   in an age of horse-carriages and wooden sail boats

departing from the Sea of Japan
reaching the West Coast of America along the Pacific current
before arriving in a sun-exposed Brisbane
when long strips of plastic islands   were
gathering   scraping past
the drifting bottle, cast a hundred years ago

right now   news from Songkhla
has just arrived that a whale, having swallowed 80 plastic bags, died
in the Andaman Sea

撕裂

把创伤 隐秘在黑暗里
先躲过闪电的追杀
灵魂以折叠的形式 储存
在每一片星云的背面

鬼魅的暗流 撕裂完
物质 银河与星系之后
肉体或将重新上路
追踪那一盏渐行渐远的天灯

Tearing

Keep the wound   a secret in the dark
first escape from the killing pursuit of a lightning
so that soul can, in a folded form   save itself
behind each and every starry cloud

after the dark currents of ghosts   finish tearing
matter   the Milky Way and the Galaxy
flesh may hit the road again
in pursuit of the sky lantern as it keeps getting further away

燃烧

目光 会接受这样的事实
色彩包裹住视线
同时肢解它

真容躲在极寒的空白处
融解化身成火
开始攻击

我不是坠入泥土与物质的深渊
是燃烧 是蒸发
是一片虚无

(2019.4.27)

Burning

The eye may accept such a fact
that colours wrap up the line of sight
while dismembering it

true features, hidden in the extremely cold blank spots
and turned into fire
begin attacking

I'm not an abyss fallen into the mud and matter
but a burning   an evaporation
a nothingness

弯曲的不仅仅是地上的河流

神在切割大地时
为天空之城　倾盆而下的雨水
保留下奔腾的千沟万壑

打开思想的切片
连接好跃动的脑电图　澎湃的激流
会划过死寂的显屏

其实　缠绕和旋转一刻也没停止
从楼顶开始　穿过肉体和混凝土的阻挡
直抵昏暗的地下室

还有　除了一排排笔直的刺刀
蜿蜒的隔离墙上　是已经凝固的血光
是鞭子或笼型铁丝网

现在我缅怀的　不仅仅
是地上弯曲的河流　还有同样散落在地上
弯曲的器官　肠子和内脏

(2019.1.26)

It's Not Only the Rivers That Are Bent

When God cuts the earth
He keeps thousands, tens of thousands, of rushing gullies and valleys
for the buckets of rainwater, from the City of Sky

when you open the slices of brain
and connect them with the leaping EEG   the upsurging torrents
will slice across the dead quiet of the screen

in fact   the windings and gyrations never stop for a moment
as they begin from the top of the building   passing through the blockage
                                                of flesh and concrete
directly reaching the gloomy basement

moreover   apart from rows of pen-straight bayonets
there, on the meandering separating walls   are lights of blood, congealed
the whips or cage-shaped barbed wire

what I now miss   are not only
the bent rivers   but also the bent organs   intestines and innards
scattered, likewise, on the ground

着陆器

你在月球的背面
一个叫冯卡门的地方着陆 打开了
另一段时间的面孔

地球上的赞美之词
略显暗淡 其实 太阳的视线在这里
早已不再重启

比起潮起和潮落
我们的呼吸是渺小的 而恒久之力
隐秘在漆黑的苍穹

(2019.1.3)

The Landing Vehicle

You landed on the backside of the moon
at a place called, 'von Kármán'   and opened
the face of another time

eulogies on the earth
seemed dim   and in fact   the vision of the sun here
no longer got restarted

compared with the ebbs and flows
our breathings are insignificant   and the power of eternity
is hidden, in the darkness of the firmament

我无法拒绝你的到来

夜深 你重新潜入我的梦
告诉我有关伯利恒 和法老的金手柄蛇仗
丢失的消息

太空行走还在继续
星星 继续缠绕着哪一块弹射的瓦片
白鸽继续在平流层下方飞行

大片肉体的热度
覆盖掉弧形的水面 覆盖掉青草的味道
野象谷遗址已经关闭

一滴泪 融化在黑色的空气里
我无法拒绝你的到来
清点完简单的行装 仅剩头颅和血

(2018.10.6)

I Can't Refuse Your Coming

Deep at night   when you, once again, come into my dream
and tell me about the loss
of the Gold Snake Handles of Bethlehem   and Pharaoh

space walks are continuing
and stars   are continuing to twine around an ejected tile
as white doves are continuing to fly under the stratosphere

the heat of masses of flesh
are covering up curvaceous water surfaces   and the smells of green grass
when the remains of the Wild Elephant Valley are closed

a single tear   melted in the black air
I can't refuse your coming
when the simple luggage is sorted out   only the head and blood are left

虫子的哲学

你可见的光
仅是一场圣宴的彩排部分
不朽的黑暗　始终
在无边的世界外游荡

虫子的哲学
是每一次爬行　都要读懂
辽阔的大地与微小的洞穴的关系
且不迷失自我

你　用短暂的时间
煮熟一只鸭子
而你的星球　用漫长的时间
煮熟你

(2018.8.19)

The Philosophy of an Insect

The light you can see
is only the rehearsal part of a sumptuous dinner
while eternal darkness   constantly
roams outside the boundless world

the philosophy of an insect
is that each time it crawls it needs to understand
the relationship of the vast land to the tiny cave
without losing itself

you   within the short time
cook a duck
but your planet   takes a long time
in cooking you

中文房间

  你可以运行一个程序
  但只能给出一个智能的印象

   — John Searle

你坐在
堆满中文笔划的房间
试图翻越燧木取火　楔形文字
和光滑的竹简
朝水墨的边沿靠近

而运行中的物体
告诉你　未来在漏斗的上方
过去在漏斗的下方
你不间断追赶闪灵　机器的利爪
始终隔着窄窄的门缝

其实　汉字的祖先
是一种漫长的搏杀兵器
常布满密道的两侧　某一天你醒来
读懂了意向的繁衍生息
这道门　才会变得虚无

(2018.8.12)

A Room of Chinese Language

    You may run a program
    But you can only give an impression of intelligence

        – John Searle

You sit
in a room piled up with Chinese strokes
trying to climb over the drilling of the wood for fire   the cuneiform script
and the smooth bamboo slips
moving close to the edge of water ink

while objects in motion
tell you   the future is above the funnel
and the past is below the funnel
you keep chasing after The Shining   the sharp claws of the machine
constantly kept outside the narrow door crack

in fact   the ancestors of Chinese characters
are a long killing machine
that often lines a secret passageway   one day when you wake up
and understand the thriving and multiplication of intentions
this door   will become nihilistic

行走在黑暗里的钟

MH370航班沉入深渊时 我听见

水下行走在黑暗里的钟 仍嘀嘀哒哒地响着

尽管时光 会准确地计算
每一寸纯净的肉体撕开 爆裂的阵痛

我知道寻找的大船 离我很近很近
也有来自遥远的呼唤 划过水的声响

这颗星球上 存在家与祖国
同时保留了隔离 苦难 迷失 分歧

可我记得更多的是温暖与相拥
还有深情的牵挂 默默的思念

或许 我会消融在指针停摆的地方
岸上清明季的花丛里 能找到我的笑容

(2014.3.30)

The Clock Walking in the Darkness

When the MH370 sank into the abyss   I heard
a clock, underwater, walking in the darkness   still ticking away

even though time   was calculating accurately
every inch of pure flesh, when torn   would erupt in pangs of pain

I know that the seeking ship   is very close to me
and there are calls from faraway   sounds crossing the waters

on this planet   there are homes and motherlands
there are also separation   suffering   losses   disagreements

but what I can remember more is warmth and embraces
deep caring   and silent longings

possibly   I'll melt where the hour hand stops
in the flowers of the Qingming season   you can find my smile

无法阻挡

一粒雨滴
从屋檐的缝隙自由滑落 紧接着
这近乎完美的姿态
瞬间瓦解

武夫的刀
不总是消磨在凄厉的风声里
有别于动物的齿印
其切口 是两个整齐的断面

吻 和繁衍
是冷血向热血的过渡仪式
是阴谋的陷阱旁 盛开不息的花
是流淌至海里的一股熔岩

鸟类的眼睛看得很远
一生的忧伤埋在漂亮的云彩中
连接近的子弹
也划出了一根美学的弧线

世界在握手 我
在聆听光线刺进泥土时的响动
此时 我的视线 无法阻挡
死盯住那张阴影的脸

(2018.6.24)

Impossible to Stop

A drop of rain
freely slipped, between the eaves   and shortly after
the near-perfect posture
disintegrated in an instant

the knife of a butcher
does not always wear down in the chilly wind
its incisions, different from the tooth marks
of the animals   are two even sections

kisses   and reproduction
are a transitional ritual from cold blood to hot
are constantly opening flowers   by the side of a trap of conspiracy
are a stream of molten lava that runs into the sea

the eyes of the birds can see far
their lifetime sorrow buried in the pretty clouds
even the approaching bullets
have drawn a line of aesthetic curve

the worlds are shaking hands   I
am listening to the sound of light as it pierces into the mud
right now   my vision   is impossible to stop
staring at the face in the shadow

渐行渐远

晚风 从太阳落下的山谷吹来
祭祀已经结束
你的紫衣 将大片的湖水染成紫色

我仅把属于天边的一抹潮红
放进我的部分章节
重新填入至空洞的笔划里

轻的纸张或墨水
可以保留时间的划痕 但承载不了
沉重的思恋与泪水

你穷尽我一生的 其实
不是带风声的动词 而是你一连串
密集的渐行渐远的闪烁

(2018.6.21)

Getting Further Away

The evening wind   was blowing from the valley where the sun is down
the sacrificial service over
your purple clothes   had caused large expanses of lake water to turn purple

I put only the trace of flushing, at the edge of the sky
in a part of my chapter
refilling the empty strokes with it

light paper or ink
can keep scratch traces of time   but it can't bear
heavy longings and tears

what you've gone through my life with   is in fact
not the verbs carrying the sound of wind   but your string
of dense flickerings, getting further away

链接 还在继续

从脸到瞳孔 再到粉红的虹膜
这些神施予的印记
会成为你的肉体
行走在另一群肉体间的识别

当然 神的手有时也离开圣坛
把咒语的一部分进行编码
标注出一串和死亡有关的图谱
并告诉你 无法逃脱的理由

拆解完你有限的骨头
或死因不详 或流干剩下的血
或将可怜的罪过 贴上一枚
标签 暂时投送至一堆泥土里

链接 是绳索的另一种宿命
继续控制 其实 没有停止的迹象
待太阳风吹皱迟到的雨季
你目光里的柔情 开始暗淡 模糊

(2017.6.13)

The Link, Still Continuing

From the face to the pupil   and further on to the pink iris
these marks, given by God
will become the sign by which to identify
your flesh walking in another crowd of fleshes

of course   God's hands sometimes depart from the altar
and encode part of the curse
putting a label on a string of diagrams related to death
and telling you   the reasons of inescapabilities

after dismantling your limited bones
it's either an unknown cause of death   or bleeding till it went dry
or putting a label   on the pitiable
guilt   before delivering it to a heap of mud

the link   is another fate of the rope
continuing to control   in fact   no signs of stopping
wait till the wind of sun crinkles the late season of rain
when the tenderness of your eyes   begins to darken   to dim

玩具屋

  妈妈：你往下看　那是什么
  小女孩：那是玩具屋

   - 题记

这是　飞往高原的航班上
年轻的妈妈与小女孩的短暂对话
我惊艳这样的视角

在小女孩的目光里　舷窗下
那一栋栋星星点点的红蓝与灰白的建筑
仍是她童话世界的一部分

我哀叹　无情的成人世界
对我眼前的岁月
套上了一副沉重的枷锁

大地之上
仍有长长的隔离墙　边境线
蛇形铁丝网　囚笼和密集的枪响

而玩具屋　没有忧愁和悲伤
我梦想着的人们　在玩具屋长大
在玩具屋生儿育女　直至终老

无论南半球还是北半球
无论富人区　还是山坡上的贫民窟
无论白色人种还是有色人种

(2018.5.6)

The Dollhouse

    Mom: Look down   what is that?
    The little girl: That's the dollhouse

        – an inscription

This is   a brief conversation between the young mother
and her daughter on board a flight towards the plateau
I am amazed by this perspective

in her eyes   and below the window
the dots of buildings, red-blue and grey-white
remain part of her fairy tale

I lament   the ruthless world of adults
as it has shackled the years in front of my eyes
with heavy chains

over the land
there are still long separating walls   the borderlines
and the serpentine barbed wire   cages and dense reports of gunshots

but in the dollhouse   there are no worries or sadness
people I dream of   are growing up there
and have kids   till they age

regardless of the southern hemisphere or the northern
regardless of the district of the rich   or the slums on the slopes
regardless of the whites or the people of colour

猫的脚步比时间的钟摆还轻

先是女人的声音来到耳畔
母体的香 乳汁和吻的画面急速回放
坏死的血 开始向心的方向收缩
右眼角 一滴清泪

留恋的面容下
是两瓣 渐渐关闭的黑郁金香的唇
柴门外 古道边
隐约的雾气里有一行举幡的人

光 变得虚无
猫的脚步比时间的钟摆还轻
风中 一张薄纸飘向悠悠的天
我知道 你是一个好人

(2018.4.30)

The Cat's Steps Always Lighter than the Pendulum

It started off with a woman's voice reaching the edge of my ear
a speedy rewind of the scenes, with the fragrance of mother's body milk and
                                                                                     kisses
necrotic blood   began contracting in the direction of heart
and, at the corner of the right eye   a single clear tear

under the longing facial features
were two lips   of black tulip, gradually closing
outside the painted door   and by the side of the ancient road
half-visibly in the blurring mist, there was a line of people holding up the
                                                                                     banners

while the light   became abstract
the cat's steps were lighter than the pendulum
in the wind   a thin piece of paper was floating towards the vast sky
and I knew   you were a good person

总想 爱这个世界多一点

枯叶下的一群虫子
没走出过一个季节的长度 岸旁
是整片消失的水草

鱼汛 准时来临
层层窒息的光 紧紧包裹住鲜艳的鳃
白皙的手 提前放在盘子的两侧

剩下的内脏 藏匿在暗下来的花园里
总想爱这个世界多一点
在我老死的面庞还未僵硬前

(2018.4.24)

Always Wanting   to Love This World a Bit More

A group of insects under the withered leaves
had not walked out of the length of a season   and by the bank
was a full spread of disappearing water grass

the fish news   arrived on time
layers of strangling light   tightly wrapped around the florid gills
pale hands   were placed on either side of the plate, ahead of time

the innards that remained   were hidden in the darkening garden
always wanting to love this world a bit more
before my face, aged to death, hardened

伸出你的手

站在 昏暗的老屋外
伸出你的手 接住从老屋的屋檐上
飘落的清明季的雨水

一股透明的死亡滑过手指
瞬间坠入泥土的低处
有一种割裂的痛 开始在身体内漫延

你艰难的收回你的视线
将沉重的眼眸低垂 好让目光里的时间
保留部分思念的色彩

你继续伸出你的手
想再次挽住 曾给你温暖的潮湿的影子
可剩下的 还是那一阵墨绿的风

(2018.4.5)

Hold Out Your Hands

Stand   outside the sombre ancient house
and hold out your hands   to receive the rain water of the Qingming season
that was drifting off the eaves of the house

a transparent death was slipping through the fingers
and, in an instant, fell onto the lower grounds of mud
as a cutting pain   began spreading itself throughout the body

you, with difficulty, retrieve your line of vision
lowering your heavy eyelids   so that time in your eyes
would retain part of the colour of longing

you keep holding out your hands
in order to once again retain   the wet shadow that once gave you warmth
but what remains   is still the dark-green wind

光年系列·圣杯

时光凝固在崩塌的隧道
圣杯滑落在没有穷尽的浓汤里 肢解的口令
来自失去伪装的暗物质

每一次重复的撕碎和切割
都是你我 无法磨灭的完整的一部分
包括已经同步的悲哀

钙化的广场上的鸽子
可以证明 这个曾熄灭的世界存在着包容
我是谁 已经不重要

(2018.3.31)

Holy Grail • the Light Year Series

Time, frozen inside the collapsed tunnel
and the holy grail has slipped into the endless pottage   the password of
dismemberment
having come from the dark matter shed of its camouflage

every repetitive ripping apart and cutting
is part of an erasable whole   that is you and me
including the synchronized sadness

the doves, on the calcified square
are evidence   that this world, extinguished, contained inclusiveness
it's no longer important   who I am

光年系列·起始

翻过一道颜色的堤坝
相对于眼睛 密集的斑斓和绚丽
顺利通过大脑的介质
伪装成欲望的同谋
已看见的其实 不是真相的全部

季节坠落的事实
以几何数聚变 跨越雨季墨绿的拐点
遍地半梦半醒的物体
迎来囚禁者发明的午夜的牢笼
梦魇开始沉入湍急的河流

正在集结的
是管状的金属和闪烁的银铠甲
宵禁的反光牌
混杂在大片暗红色的空气里
出逃的路口被断崖封死

表针精密重叠
待到恢复平静时 声音的绝响
收集在整齐的器皿中
世纪的尘土 分别标明光年的起始
需要寻找的是来世的重生

(2018.3.20)

The Beginnings • the Light Year Series

When you climb over an embankment of colours
relative to the eye   dense gorgeousness and magnificence
have camouflaged themselves as conspirators of desire
through the brain matter
what is seen is in fact   not the whole truth

the fallen facts of the season
experience fusion in geometric numbers   crossing the dark-green inflection
                                        point of a rainy season
objects, half-dreamy and half-awake, all over the place
are welcoming the midnight's prison, invented by the prisoners
as nightmares are sinking into a rushing river

what are gathering
are tube-like metal and shining silver armour
the reflective billboard at curfew
got mixed in the vast masses of dark-red air
as the escape routes are blocked by the broken cliff

the watch hands overlap with accuracy
when quietness is recovered   the absolute sound
is gathered inside the even utensils
the dust of the century   marked with the beginning of the light year
needs to seek for the rebirth of another world

开始融化

三月　太阳光
由南向北密集移动　先从赤道下手
进行垂直切割

我脚下的山峦　沟壑
开始滑动　紧接着是雪山的投降
透明的液态水涌出

较早惊醒的是啮齿类动物
尔后是食肉类动物　暴走的生灵
和一群我曾熟悉的山鬼

(2017.3.11)

Beginning to Melt

In March   the sunlight
was moving, densely, from south to north   starting from the equator
cutting vertically

the valley   and the mountain under my feet
began slipping   closely followed by the surrender of the snow mountain
when the transparent liquid water came surging out

those who awoke earlier were the rodents
then the meat-eaters   people of the Bosozoku kind
and a group of mountain devils I was familiar with

有一双眼睛停在我的左脸

夜携风的刀子
把天空划成一块块碎片
冷从血开始 冰冻我的手
我的脚 我的筋骨

来自黑暗雪地的亡灵
告诉我 今晚我是狩猎场里唯一的猎物
外滩 明珠塔 人行天桥已经钙化
夺路与抵抗只是缓慢的坠落

我听见耳语的叛徒
在讨论肢解我的方式 也听见
财富和荣耀 在我的灵与肉中消融的脚步
而一场热的汗 便是一场高烧的雨

此时 有一双眼睛
停在我的左脸 还有一阵轻柔的呼吸
紧贴我二尺宽的梦境 我知道
这是我温暖的女人 在为我招魂

(2011.2.3)

There Was a Pair of Eyes Stopped on My Face

The night, carrying the knives of wind
was cutting the sky into bits and pieces
when the cold began from the blood   freezing my hands
my feet   and my bones

the soul of someone dead, from the dark snow ground
told me   that tonight I was the only prey in the hunting ground
the Bund   The Pearl Tower   and the Overpass had all calcified
taking the road or resisting was but a slow fall

I heard the whispering traitors
discussing ways of dissecting me   and I also heard
the melting footsteps of fortune and glory   in my soul and flesh
whereas a hot shower of sweat   was a highly feverish rain

right now   there was a pair of eyes
stopped on the left side of my face   and a soft breathing
close to my two-feet-wide dream   and I knew
it was my warm woman   calling for my soul

你一直在哪里

你的拯救　用无形的利器包裹
可摧毁一路坚硬的屏障
包括一个星河　阻隔
另一个星河的宇宙墙

你在数字与文字的空隙里
填充进八卦与占星术
再把神的语言一篇又一篇
重复　天堂之门的存在

你从刀耕火种到原子核变
从一枚成功的卵子到太阳季的风暴
从流寇到帝都的满城旌旗
从死亡　到最后上演的重生

你始终在令我们作出选择
或堕落　或占有　或驱逐与被驱逐
或一群生命发动对另一群生命的讨伐
连孤独的狼群　也不得不选择

不论时光的长河流淌多久
不论末日将至是否来临
也不论祈祷的祭坛献上多少颗头颅
其实　你一直在哪里

(2018.2.19)

Where Have You Been?

Your salvation   wrapped up with shapeless weapons
could destroy a road of hard barriers
including the stoppage   of a galaxy
the universal wall of another galaxy

in the gap between figures and words, you
filled the eight trigrams and astrology
and repeated   the existence of the Gate to Heaven
with one article after another in God's language

you moved from slashing and burning to nuclear changes
from a successful egg to the storm of the sun's season
from a roving rebel to the flags filling the capital of the empire
and from death   to the rebirth in the final performance

you have always made us make a choice
to either fall   to possess   to expel   or to be expelled
or to cause group of lives to crusade against another group
when even the lone wolves   had to make a choice

however long the river of time flowed
whether the end of the world was forthcoming
and regardless how many heads there were at the altar of prayers
you have always been there   in fact

物质的边沿

是滑落 隔离与荒凉
是拉长或挤压的双腿 还有
残喘 贫贱的影子

等一层薄的日光暗下来
戴面具的黑衣人立在风的入口处
收缴你的籍贯和身份

必须出售的能量
是归途 是付给远方盘缠的一部分
剩下的会重新排工 筛选

用积攒的金币献给天堂
用挥洒的汗水 滋养地狱的花草
寒冷 终是囚禁了温暖

(2017.11.29)

At the Edge of the Matter

are slippage   separation and desolation
are elongating or compressed legs   and also
the gasping   impoverished shadows

when a layer of thin sunshine darkens
the man in black clothes, wearing a facemask, stands at the entrance to the wind
and confiscates the place of your birth and your identity

the energy that must be sold
is journey home   a portion of the money for it that is paid for distances
what remains will have to be resorted   screened

the accumulated gold coins are to be contributed to heavens
the scattered sweat is to be   nourishing the flowers and grasses of hell
but coldness   has ended up imprisoning the warmth

剥开一枚果壳

我 在另外一个星球
剥开一枚果壳
这里的季风 是种子的襁褓

词汇和语言
储存在山冈或凹地的灌木丛
水隐没于流动的岩层

沿途孕育的子宫
随花的信使
接管生命的轮回和陨落

眼睛和泪滴
已经摆脱了忧伤和苦痛
光线均匀地打在额头

(2017.8.3)

Opening the Shell of a Fruit

I   on another planet
am opening the shell of a fruit
the monsoon here   is the swaddle of the seed

words and language
are stored in the hill or the undergrowth in the hollow
while water is hidden in the flowing rock strata

the wombs, gestating along the way
and following the messenger of the flowers
takes over the transmigration and falls of life

eyes and tears
have rid themselves of sorrow and bitter pain
while light is, evenly, striking the forehead

我弯曲地寄生在你肉体的深处

我诞生在星云 水气和石头之前
几乎用无形的身段在这个世界繁衍

我的行动可以超级至吞噬你的无知
对于我 死亡是一道芳香的味觉的圣宴

我的痛处和孤寂按几何数列阵
外面的万古江山装不下我的思想

我的王国 在时间的谷底 黑暗的边沿
这儿密集的屠戮 超过了雨点的数量

启示录 告诉我飞禽走兽的踪迹
我一次又一次封存消逝与重生的讯息

而我弯曲地寄生在你肉体的深处
是在等待 再等待又一场沉重的别离

(2018.1.27)

I, Bent, Lived in the Depths of Your Body, Like a Parasite

Born before the star cloud   water airs and stones, I
was multiplying in this world, almost with a shapeless figure

my action could be so superior that it would swallow up your ignorance
and for me   death was a sumptuous dinner of fragrant tastebuds

my painful spots and solitude were geometrically arrayed
so that the mountains and rivers, from time immemorial, couldn't contain my
thoughts

my kingdom   at the bottom of the valley   and at the edge of darkness
where intensified butcherings   have exceeded the number of raindrops

The Book of Revelation   told me of the traces of animals and birds
but I, again and again, sealed off the information about vanishment and rebirth

and I, bent, lived in the depths of your body, like a parasite
am waiting   again for a heavy departure

梦山

其实 一直耸立在我的心里
那儿埋葬了我的爱恋 和前世的姻缘

我曾用山火取暖
用叮咚叮咚的清泉冲洗霉烂的交媾

我不放过山上的一草一木
挥霍掉所有同山有关的雨露 白云
包括一弯新月

我奸杀后山的蓝狐
捣毁经常有仙出没的悠深的洞穴

后来我一无所有 赤身裸体
漂浮在山脚 即将干枯的湖面

我听见秃鹰震颤的翅膀
从天空的缝隙里 俯冲下来

我的灵与肉　　以及残存的憧憬
一点一滴消逝在 后退的山的阴影中

(2013.5.25)

The Dream Mountain

In fact   has been standing tall in my heart
where my love is buried   along with a marriage of a previous life

I used to get warm over a mountain fire
and wash the rotten copulation with the tinkling clean spring

I did not let go of grass or trees there
and I laid waste to the dew or the white clouds   related to the mountain
including a crescent

I raped the blue fox on the back of the mountain
I destroyed the deep cave where deities frequented

subsequently I was left with nothing   in the nude
floating at the foot of the mountain   on the drying lake

I heard the trembling wings of a bald-headed eagle
swooping   from the seam of the sky

my soul and my flesh as well as what remained of my longing
was disappearing, bit by bit   in the shadow of the receding mountain

远方走来一位失明的歌者

没有 歌词和完整的韵律
从喉咙深处发出的
是长啸或雄鸡的嘶鸣
是森林和山谷苏醒的声音

黑暗的大湖边 一圈圈
舞蹈的裙摆在碎波上跃动
篝火的遗址保留烈焰的痕迹
风的手鼓 不停的打击

语言和肢体的表达
在危险和仇恨的旷野播洒
刀光穿过密集的雨点
一路追杀 向西逃的亡灵

坚韧古老的岩石上
涂满了大片祭献的音符
虎豹在前 狼群在后
白骨与骷髅填没整个守猎场

(2018.1.10)

A Blind Singer Came from Afar

There were no   lyrics or complete rhythms
what was issuing from the depths of the throat
was the long roar or the croaking of a pheasant
was the sound of the forest and mountains waking up

by the side of the big dark lake   rings
of skirt hemlines were leaping over the broken wavelets
ruins of a bonfire had kept the traces of fiery flames
the tambourine of wind   kept beating

the expression of language and limbs
was scattering across the wilderness of danger and hate
and the light of a knife, through the dense raindrops
was pursuing   the dead souls running westward

the firm and ancient rock
was smeared with huge masses of sacrificial musical notes
tigers and leopards in front   packs of wolves behind
the hunting ground was filled with white bones and skeletons

她的盛装还是那样艳丽

当坚硬的物质世界深睡时
我知道 我的外婆
正从没有重量的梦境走来

记忆在平行的空间延伸
银河 投射在青绿的坟茔上
死亡是她在门里我在门外

可她的盛装还是那样艳丽
蓝袄 金丝的边扣
还有脚底 黑缎小脚的帖鞋

(2017.12.14)

Her Finery Was Still So Gorgeous

When the world of hard matter was profoundly asleep
I knew   my Grandma
was coming from a weightless dream

memory was extending itself in a parallel space
the Milky Way   was reflected on the green grave
death was her, inside the door, and I was outside

but her finery was still so gorgeous
her blue robe   gold-threaded side-buttons
and her soles   in the tiny-footed shoes of black satin

核

在众神愤怒前
核　是一切果实的中心
是活下去的理由

自切尔诺贝利的泪滴落
和福岛海岸
这苍凉的浪花　翻腾

有毒的蘑菇云
虽没有准时升起
菊与刀的故事却没有停止

在东半球或西半球
我无法判断　谁将点爆
最后一秒临界值

我只想
第一时间推开庙门　为明天
找到一个不死的答案

(2017.2.18)

Nuclear

Before the fury of all the gods
nuclear   is the centre of all fruit
the reason to survive

tears drop off Chernobyl
and Fukushima
these vast wave-flowers   churning

although the poisonous mushroom clouds
did not rise on time
the story of chrysanthemum and swords never stops

in the eastern or western hemisphere
I can hardly judge   who will explode
the threshold of the final second

all I'm thinking is
push open the door of the temple first thing   to find an undying answer
for tomorrow

www.ingramcontent.com/pod-product-compliance
Lightning Source LLC
Chambersburg PA
CBHW030949090426
42737CB00007B/554